W9-ASL-407

DATE DUE

970   BC#34880000025721 $25.36
FOX   Fox, Mary Virginia
        North America

Morrill E.S.
Chicago Public Schools
1431 North Leamington Avenue
Chicago, IL 60651

CONTINENTS

North America

Mary Virginia Fox

Heinemann Library
Chicago, Illinois

Designed by Joanna Hinton-Malivoire and Q2A Creative
Printed in China by South China Printing Company

10 09 08 07 06
10 9 8 7 6 5 4 3 2 1

New edition ISBN: 1-4034-8544-5 (hardcover)
                           1-4034-8552-6 (paperback)

The Library of Congress has cataloged the first edition as follows:
Fox, Mary Virginia.
        North America / Mary Virginia Fox.
                p. cm. – (Continents)
        Includes bibliographical references (p.) and index.
        ISBN 1-58810-001-4
        1. North America–Juvenile literature. [1. North America.] I. Title.
II. Continents (Chicago, Ill.)
E38.5 .F695 2001
970–dc21

                                                        00-011469

Acknowledgments
The publishers are grateful to the following for permission to reproduce copyright material:
Getty Images/Robert Harding World Imagery/R H Productions, 5, Bruce Coleman, Inc./Dr. Eckart Pott, p. 7; Earth Scenes/S. Osolinski, p. 9; Bruce Coleman, Inc./Bob Burch, p. 11; Corbis/Scott T. Smith, p. 13; Bruce Coleman, Inc/M.P.L. Fogden, p. 14; Bruce Coleman, Inc./Ed Degginger, p. 15; Bruce Coleman, Inc./Peter French, p. 16; Bruce Coleman, Inc./Keith Gunnar, p. 17; Bruce Coleman, Inc./ J. Sarapochiello, p. 19; Tony Stone/Joseph Pobereskin, p. 21; Bruce Coleman, Inc./Sharon Smith, p. 22; Tony Stone/Donald Nausbaum, p. 23; Earth Scenes/Eastcott/Momotiak/p. 24; Bruce Coleman, Inc./ J.C. Carton, p. 25; Photo Edit/Myrleen Ferguson, p. 27; Tony Stone/Doug Armand, p. 28; Photo Edit/Cindy Charles, p. 29.

Cover photograph of North America, reproduced with permission of Science Photo Library/ Tom Van Sant, Geosphere Project/ Planetary Visions.

The publishers would like to thank Kathy Peltan, Keith Lye, and Nancy Harris for their assistance in the preparation of this book.

Every effort has been made to contact copyright holders of any material reproduced in this book. Any omissions will be rectified in subsequent printings if notice is given to the publisher.

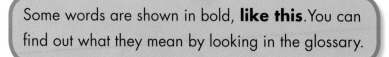

Some words are shown in bold, **like this**. You can find out what they mean by looking in the glossary.

Contents

Where Is North America? 4

Weather 6

Mountains and Deserts 8

Rivers 10

Lakes 12

Animals 14

Plants 16

Languages 18

Cities 20

In the Country 24

Famous Places 26

Fast Facts 30

Glossary *31*

More Books to Read *32*

Index *32*

Where Is North America?

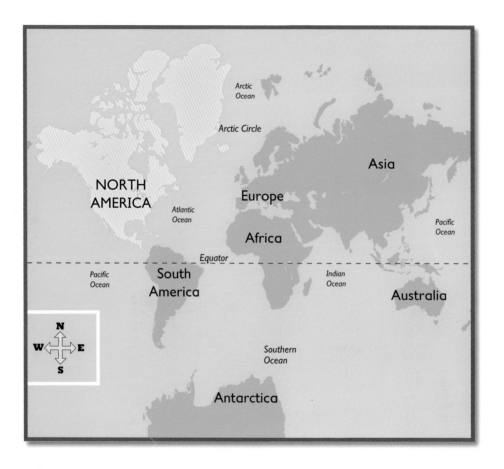

There are seven continents. A continent is a very large area of land. North America is the third largest continent. It stretches north beyond the **Arctic Circle**. In the south, a narrow strip of land connects North and South America.

On either side of North America, there are two great oceans. To the west is the Pacific Ocean. To the east is the Atlantic Ocean. North America includes many islands. Some of these islands belong to countries that are in other continents.

Greenland is part of the continent of North America, but it belongs to Denmark, in Europe.

▲ *The large island of Greenland is in the Arctic Ocean.*

Weather

North America has many different
climates. In the south, the weather is very
warm and it often rains. In the southwest,
there are hot **deserts**. Along the west coast,
the sun shines most of the time.

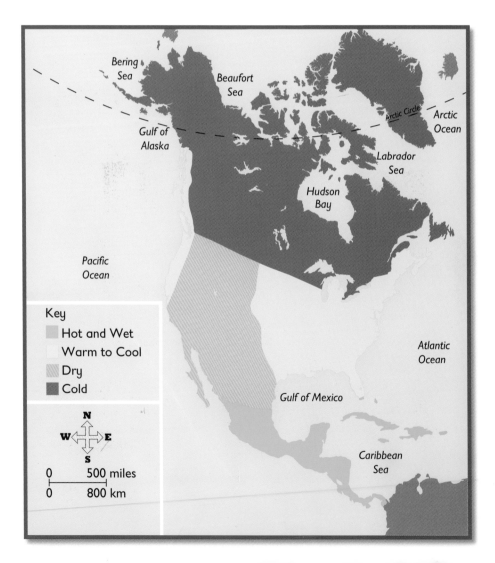

Bering Sea

Beaufort Sea

Arctic Circle

Arctic Ocean

Gulf of Alaska

Labrador Sea

Hudson Bay

Pacific Ocean

Atlantic Ocean

Key
- Hot and Wet
- Warm to Cool
- Dry
- Cold

Gulf of Mexico

N
W E
S

0   500 miles
0   800 km

Caribbean Sea

▲ *This frozen ground is in northern Canada.*

Near the **Arctic Circle**, the ground stays frozen all year. The northwest coast is cool and rainy. But in much of North America, it is cold and snowy in the winter and hot in the summer.

Mountains and Deserts

There are high mountain **ranges** along the west of North America. The Rocky Mountains go from the **deserts** of Mexico to icy Alaska. The Appalachian Mountains in the east are older and lower than the Rocky Mountains.

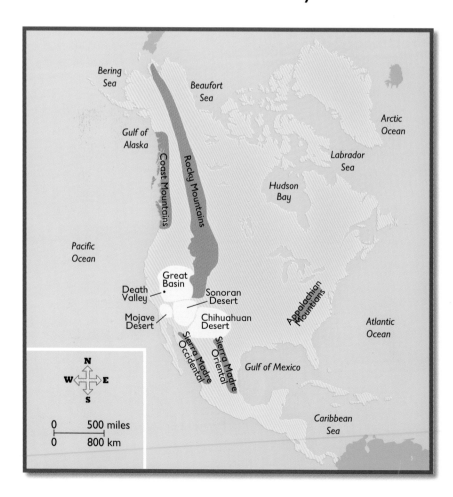

This dry, stony desert is hot in the day and cold at night.

▲ *This is the Sonoran Desert in New Mexico.*

There are several large deserts in the southwestern United States and Mexico. Death Valley is a desert in California. It is the hottest place in the United States. The temperature there has reached 135 °F (57 °C).

Rivers

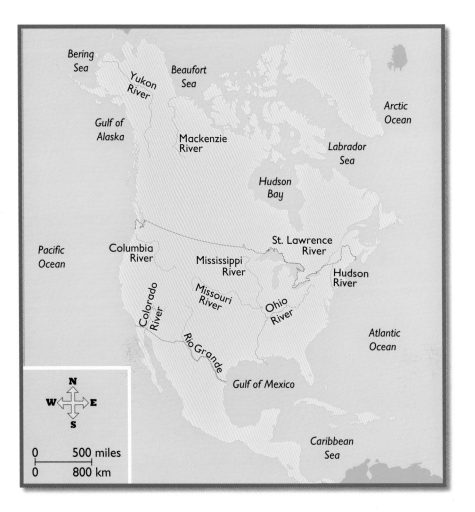

The Mississippi is one of the world's most important rivers. It starts near the Canadian **border**. It then flows south through the center of the United States. Two other great rivers, the Missouri and the Ohio, run into the Mississippi.

The St. Lawrence River runs eastward from the Great Lakes to the Atlantic Ocean. Large ocean-going ships can travel along the river because **canals** take ships safely from one place to another.

▲ *Ships travel along canals on the St. Lawrence River.*

Lakes

There are five large **freshwater** lakes close to the **border** of the United States and Canada. They are called the Great Lakes. The lakes are linked to each other by **canals**, so large ships can travel between them.

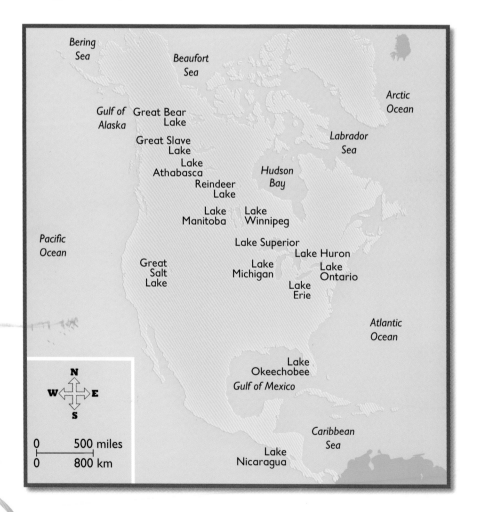

Bering Sea

Beaufort Sea

Arctic Ocean

Gulf of Alaska

Great Bear Lake

Great Slave Lake

Labrador Sea

Lake Athabasca

Reindeer Lake

Hudson Bay

Lake Manitoba

Lake Winnipeg

Pacific Ocean

Lake Superior

Lake Huron

Great Salt Lake

Lake Michigan

Lake Ontario

Lake Erie

Atlantic Ocean

Lake Okeechobee

Gulf of Mexico

N
W E
S

0   500 miles
0   800 km

Caribbean Sea

Lake Nicaragua

▲ *This is the Great Salt Lake, in Utah.*

The Great Salt Lake is a **shallow** lake in a **desert**. It is in Utah, in the western United States. Its water is very salty. Swimmers can easily float in it.

Animals

Millions of buffalo, also called bison, used to live on the grassy **plains** of North America. Golden eagles and pumas live in the mountains of the north. Alligators and turtles lurk in the **swamps** of Florida, in the southern United States.

▼ *These buffalo live in a national park in South Dakota.*

Most buffalo live in **national parks**. This protects them from hunters.

▲ *Polar bears live in the Arctic.*

Polar bears live in the frozen north of the continent. They hunt for fish where there are breaks in the ice. Whales, walruses, and seals swim in the icy Arctic Sea.

Plants

Redwoods are the tallest trees in the world. Some reach up to 367 feet (112 meters) tall.

▲ *These redwood trees are in California.*

Giant redwood trees grow on the northwest coast of the United States. Maple trees grow in Canada and the northeast of the United States. In spring, people use the **sap** from inside the trees to make maple syrup.

Many types of cactuses grow in the **deserts** of the southwest. Saguaro cactuses are very tough. They need very little water to survive.

Saguaro cactuses can be as tall as a four-story building.

▲ *Saguaro cactuses are found in Mexico.*

Languages

The first people living in North America were **Native Americans**. They had their own languages. Now, only a few Native Americans use these languages. Most people in the United States speak English. There are also many people who speak Spanish.

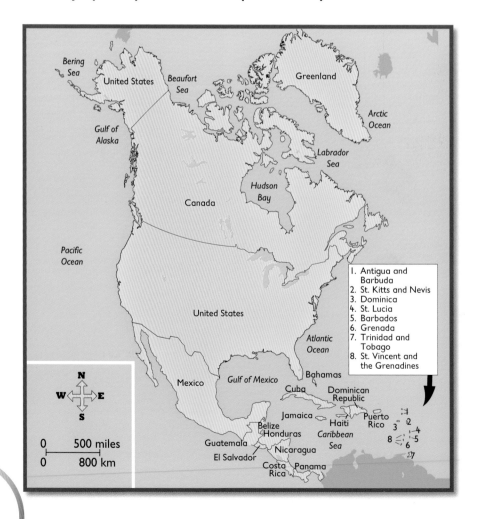

▲ *This is Oaxaca City, Mexico.*

The area south of the United States is called
Central America. Most people in Central
America speak Spanish. In Canada, some
people speak French and some speak English.

Cities

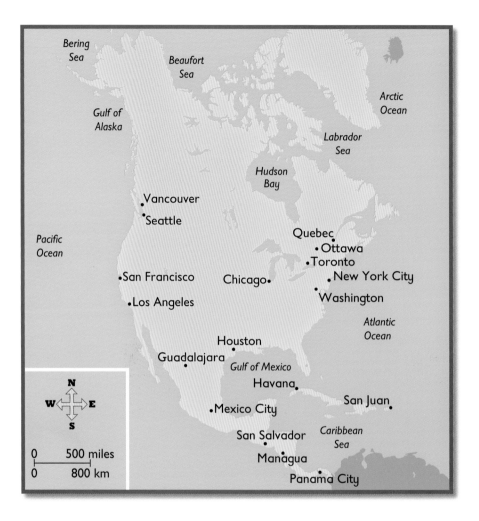

Bering Sea
Beaufort Sea
Gulf of Alaska
Arctic Ocean
Labrador Sea
Hudson Bay
Vancouver
Seattle
Quebec
Ottawa
Toronto
Pacific Ocean
San Francisco
Chicago
New York City
Los Angeles
Washington
Atlantic Ocean
Houston
Guadalajara
Gulf of Mexico
Havana
N
W   E
S
Mexico City
San Juan
0   500 miles
0   800 km
San Salvador
Caribbean Sea
Managua
Panama City

This map shows some of the main cities in the continent of North America. Toronto, in Canada, is a busy **port** on Lake Ontario. Ottawa is the **capital city** of Canada. The Canadian **parliament** meets there.

20

In the United States, New York City is one of the most important cities in the world. People from all over the world visit the city for business and fun. New York City is famous for its tall skyscrapers.

▲ *Skyscrapers fill New York City.*

Mexico City, Mexico, is the largest city in North America. It is an important business center. It has many modern buildings. It also has lots of churches built by Spanish **settlers**.

The ruins of an ancient city, built by the **Aztecs**, lie under Mexico City.

▲ *This building is in Mexico City.*

Havana was built by Spanish settlers about 500 years ago.

▲ *This picture shows Havana, Cuba.*

Havana is the **capital city** of Cuba. Cuba is the biggest island in the Caribbean Sea. Havana is a lively center for jazz musicians and singers. It sells cigars, sugar, coffee, and fruit to other countries.

In the Country

▲ *Farmers harvest wheat in Alberta, Canada.*

North America has many types of countryside. In the center are **plains** covered with wheat fields. Near the coasts, farmers raise cattle. In forests in Canada, **lumberjacks** cut down trees and saw them into logs.

On the northeast coast, people go fishing for cod and mackerel. In the countries around the Caribbean Sea, the **climate** is good for growing coffee, sugar, and bananas.

▲ *This man picks bananas in Costa Rica.*

Famous Places

Yellowstone National Park is the oldest **national park** in the world. The park contains hundreds of geysers. Geysers are jets of hot steam that shoot up suddenly out of the ground.

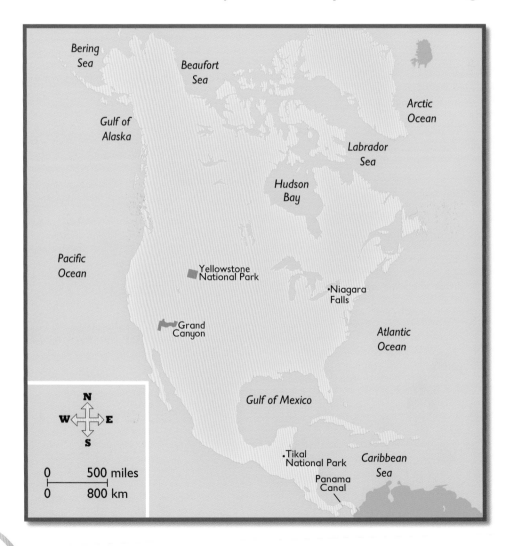

The Grand Canyon is 277 miles (446 km) long.

▲ *The Grand Canyon is in Arizona.*

The Grand Canyon is a very steep, rocky river valley in Arizona. It was formed over millions of years by the Colorado River. The river water cut through the layers of rock to make this deep canyon.

Niagara Falls forms part of the **border** between the United States and Canada.

▲ *This part of Niagara Falls is in Canada.*

Niagara Falls is made up of two big waterfalls. The American Falls are in the United States, in New York. The Horseshoe Falls are in Canada. Boats take visitors close to the crashing water.

The Maya people lived in Central America about 800 years ago. They built stone cities in forests. At the center of these cities were **temples** shaped like pyramids.

The Maya people had their own way of writing. They used picture symbols.

▲ *This Mayan pyramid is in Tikal, Guatemala.*

Fast Facts

North America's longest rivers

Name of river	Length in miles	Length in kilometers	Begins	Ends
Missouri	2,540	4,087	Rocky Mountains	Mississippi River
Mississippi	2,350	3,781	Northwest Minnesota	Gulf of Mexico
Yukon	1,979	3,184	Canada	Bering Sea

North America's highest mountains

Name of mountain	Range	Height in feet	Height in meters	Country or U.S. State
Mount McKinley	Alaska Range	20,320	6,194	Alaska
Mount Whitney	Sierra Nevada	14,494	4,418	California
Mount Elbert	Rocky Mountains	14,439	4,401	Colorado

North America's record breakers

The **border** between Canada and the United States is the world's longest land border.

Lake Superior, on the border of Canada and the United States, is the world's largest **freshwater** lake.

The Great Salt Lake in Utah is saltier than the oceans.

The Mississippi, Missouri, and Ohio rivers join to form the third largest river system in the world. It is 3,877 miles (6,236 kilometers) long.

Glossary

Arctic Circle imaginary line that circles Earth near the North Pole

Aztecs people who lived in Mexico about 500 years ago

border dividing line between one country and another

canal large human-made channel filled with water that ships and boats travel through

capital city city where government leaders work

climate type of weather a place has

desert hot, dry place with very little rain

freshwater water that is not salty

lumberjack someone who cuts down trees and saws them into logs

national park area of wild land protected by the government

Native Americans first people to live in North America

parliament name used in some countries for the group of people who make the laws of the country

plain large, flat area of land

port town or city with a harbor, where ships come and go

range line mountains that are connected to each other

sap sugary liquid inside a plant or tree

settler person who comes to live in a country

shallow not very deep

swamp very wet, muddy land

temple place built to worship a god or goddess

More Books to Read

Kite, L. Patricia. *Watching Bison in North America*. Chicago: Heinemann Library, 2006.

Parker, Vic. *We're from Mexico*. Chicago: Heinemann Library, 2006.

Whitehouse, Patricia. *Plains*. Chicago: Heinemann Library, 2005.

Index

animals 14, 15

Arctic Circle 4, 7, 15

Canada 7, 19, 20, 24, 28, 30

canals 11, 12

Central America 19, 29

cities 20, 21, 22, 23

climate 6, 25

countryside 24

deserts 6, 8, 9, 13

islands 5

lakes 12, 13, 30

languages 18, 19

Mexico 8, 9, 19, 22

mountains 8

Native Americans 18

oceans 5

plants 16, 17

rivers 10, 11, 27

Rocky Mountains 8

South America 4

weather 6, 7, 9